Compl

Travel Guide

Aziz Barakat

Copyright ©

Aziz Barakat

© 2023 UAE

Table of Contents

Introduction

Greetings, fellow adventurers, and welcome to the "Comprehensive Dubai Travel Guide," your gateway to an enchanting realm where modernity dances with tradition, and the allure of the desert meets the shimmering embrace of the Arabian Gulf.

Within these pages, we invite you to embark on an odyssey through the heart of one of the world's most captivating destinations – Dubai, where the extraordinary becomes ordinary, and the ordinary becomes extraordinary.

Discover Dubai's Multifaceted Splendor:

Dubai, a city that needs no introduction yet constantly surprises, captivates, and inspires. Our travel guide is more than just a compendium of attractions; it's a narrative woven into the very fabric of this dynamic metropolis.

From the iconic skyline that graces the cityscape to the hidden gems tucked away in historic districts, we invite you to peel back the layers and explore the multifaceted splendor that defines Dubai.

Guiding You Through a Tapestry of Experiences:

As your trusted travel companion, our guide goes beyond the surface, immersing you in the vibrant tapestry of Dubai's experiences. Whether you seek the adrenaline rush of desert adventures, the tranquility of pristine beaches, the thrill of world-class shopping, or the warmth of Emirati hospitality, each chapter unfolds a new facet of Dubai's rich and diverse offerings.

For Every Traveler, A Chapter Unveiled:

Tailored for all types of travelers – be it the intrepid explorer, the luxury seeker, the family on a cultural journey, or the solo wanderer craving serenity – our guide provides a roadmap to craft your own Dubai narrative.

Delve into the historic allure of Old Dubai's narrow alleys, bask in the modern splendors of Downtown, or find tranquility in the desert sands – the choice is yours.

Beyond the Now:

In this edition, we not only explore Dubai as it stands but also gaze into the future, uncovering the latest trends, innovations, and upcoming gems that are set to redefine the Dubai experience.

From avant-garde architectural wonders to culinary delights that tantalize the taste buds, we present a guide that is not just current but also forward-thinking.

So, fellow wanderers, whether you are a first-time visitor or a returning friend, let the "Comprehensive Dubai Travel Guide" be your compass in this city of dreams.

Join us on a journey that transcends time and space, where each page is a step closer to unlocking the secrets, stories, and splendors that make Dubai a destination like no other. Your adventure awaits – let's embark on it together.

Planning Your Trip- Best Time to Visit

Choosing the best time to visit Dubai is crucial for experiencing the city in its full glory. Dubai's climate is characterized by extremes, with scorching summers and milder winters.

Here's a breakdown of the seasons to help you decide the best time for your visit:

Winter (November to March):

Temperature: Winter is the most pleasant time to visit, with daytime temperatures ranging from 20°C to 30°C (68°F to 86°F).

Activities: This season is ideal for outdoor activities, beach days, and exploring the city's attractions comfortably. It's the peak tourist season, so expect more crowds and higher prices.

Spring (March to May):

Temperature: Spring sees a gradual increase in temperature, with daytime highs ranging from 25°C to 35°C (77°F to 95°F).

Activities: Spring is a good time for various outdoor activities before the scorching summer heat sets in. It's also a shoulder season, meaning you might find more moderate prices and fewer crowds compared to winter.

Summer (June to September):

Temperature: Summer is extremely hot, with daytime temperatures often exceeding 40°C (104°F) and high humidity.

Activities: While indoor attractions, shopping malls, and water parks remain popular during this time, outdoor activities can be challenging due to the intense heat.

Summer is considered the low tourist season, and you may find discounts on accommodations and activities.

Fall (September to November):

Temperature: Fall sees a gradual decrease in temperature, with daytime highs ranging from 30°C to 40°C (86°F to 104°F).

Activities: As the weather becomes more comfortable, outdoor activities become more enjoyable. Fall is a good time for sightseeing, desert excursions, and water activities. Prices and crowds start to pick up as the tourist season approaches.

Factors to Consider:

Events and Festivals: Consider visiting during events like the Dubai Shopping Festival (January-February) or the Dubai Food Festival (February-March) if you want to experience the city's vibrant cultural scene.

Ramadan: Note that Ramadan's timing changes each year based on the Islamic calendar. During this month, some attractions and restaurants may have altered hours, and it's important to respect local customs.

In summary, the best time to visit Dubai is during the winter months (November to March) if you prefer milder temperatures and a wide range of outdoor activities. However, each season offers a unique experience, so choose based on your preferences and priorities for your Dubai adventure.

Visa Requirements

Navigating the visa requirements is a crucial aspect of planning your trip to Dubai. The process may vary depending on your nationality and the purpose of your visit.

Visa Types:

Tourist Visa: For individuals visiting Dubai for leisure purposes.

Business Visa: For those traveling for business-related activities.

Transit Visa: For passengers transiting through Dubai.

Visa-Free Countries:

Citizens of certain countries do not require a visa to enter Dubai for a specified period.

This is typically for short stays, such as tourism or business meetings. However, the duration of visa-free stays can vary.

Visa on Arrival:

Some nationalities are eligible for a visa on arrival, allowing travelers to obtain a visa upon reaching Dubai International Airport. Again, the duration may vary.

Advance Visa Application:

For longer stays or specific purposes like employment, it's often necessary to apply for a visa in advance.

Visit the official website of the UAE government or contact the UAE embassy or consulate in your country for the latest visa requirements and application procedures.

Documentation:

Passport: Ensure your passport is valid for at least six months from the date of entry.

- Passport-sized photographs.
- Completed visa application form.
- Flight itinerary.
- Hotel reservation details.
- Proof of financial means to cover your stay.

Visa Application Process:

Online Application: Many visa applications can be completed online through the official channels.

In-Person Application: Some visa types may require submitting documents in person at the UAE embassy or consulate.

Fees:

Visa fees may apply and vary depending on the type and duration of the visa.

Special Circumstances:

If you plan to work or study in Dubai, specific visa categories and additional requirements may apply.

Changes and Updates:

Visa regulations are subject to change. Regularly check with official sources or consult with the UAE embassy for the latest updates before planning your trip.

Always ensure that you begin the visa application process well in advance of your planned travel dates to allow for any processing delays. It's advisable to double-check the requirements closer to your travel date for the most accurate information.

It's essential to check with the official authorities or the nearest UAE embassy for the most up-to-date information. However, here's a general overview of Dubai's visa requirements:

Budgeting and Currency Exchange

Understanding budgeting and currency exchange is essential when planning a trip to Dubai.

The city offers a range of experiences for various budgets, and having a clear understanding of currency exchange rates and local expenses will help you manage your finances effectively.

Here's a comprehensive guide to budgeting and currency exchange for your Dubai travel:

Currency:

The official currency of Dubai and the United Arab Emirates (UAE) is the UAE Dirham (AED).

Currency Exchange:

Currency exchange services are widely available at airports, banks, hotels, and exchange offices across Dubai.

It's advisable to compare rates at different locations to get the best deal. However, be cautious of hidden fees or unfavorable exchange rates.

Consider using local ATMs to withdraw cash. This is often a convenient and cost-effective option.

Exchange Rates:

Exchange rates can fluctuate. Stay informed about the current rates, and consider using reliable currency conversion apps or websites.

Credit Cards:

Credit cards are widely accepted in Dubai, especially in hotels, restaurants, and shopping malls.

Visa and MasterCard are commonly used, and American Express and Diners Club are also accepted but less frequently.

Inform your bank about your travel dates to avoid any issues with card transactions.

Budgeting for Accommodation:

Dubai offers a range of accommodation options, from luxury hotels to budget-friendly alternatives.

Prices vary, so research and book accommodations based on your budget and preferences.

Consider staying in areas outside the city center for more affordable options.

Dining Expenses:

Dining in Dubai can range from budget-friendly street food to high-end restaurants. Set a daily food budget and explore a mix of local and international cuisines.

Look for local markets and eateries for authentic and economical dining experiences.

Transportation Costs:

Dubai has an efficient public transportation system, including the metro, buses, and taxis. Calculate transportation costs based on your planned activities and use of public transport.

Entrance Fees and Attractions:

Research entrance fees for attractions, museums, and entertainment venues in advance. Some may offer discounted rates for online bookings or during specific times.

Shopping:

Dubai is known for its shopping, from luxury brands to traditional souks. Set a shopping budget and explore various markets for unique finds.

Miscellaneous Expenses:

Factor in additional costs such as travel insurance, SIM cards, and guided tours when budgeting for your trip.

Emergencies:

Keep a portion of your budget for emergencies or unexpected expenses.

Value-Added Tax (VAT):

Dubai imposes a 5% VAT on goods and services. Factor this into your budget when making purchases.

By carefully planning and budgeting for various aspects of your trip, you can ensure a fulfilling experience in Dubai without overspending. Regularly check exchange rates and stay updated on any changes to local fees or taxes.

Packing Tips

Packing for your trip to Dubai requires careful consideration of the climate, cultural norms, and the activities you plan to engage in. Here are comprehensive packing tips to ensure you are well-prepared for your visit:

Clothing:

Lightweight Fabrics: Given the warm climate, pack lightweight and breathable fabrics such as cotton and linen.

Modesty Considerations: While Dubai is modern, it's advisable to respect local customs. Women may want to pack conservative clothing for visits to religious sites.

Swimwear: If you plan to visit the beaches or pools, pack appropriate swimwear.

Footwear:

Comfortable Shoes: Dubai involves a fair amount of walking, so bring comfortable shoes suitable for exploring. Sandals and breathable shoes are ideal for warmer months.

Weather Protection:

Sunscreen: Given the strong sunlight, pack a high SPF sunscreen to protect your skin.

Hat and Sunglasses: These items provide additional protection against the sun.

Modesty Accessories:

Scarves or Shawls: Women may want to carry a scarf or shawl to cover shoulders when entering religious sites.

Long-sleeved Clothing: A light long-sleeved shirt or blouse can be useful for additional coverage.

Electronics:

Universal Adapter: Dubai uses the British-style Type G electrical outlets, so bring a universal adapter for your electronic devices.

Camera: Capture the stunning cityscape and attractions.

Personal Hygiene and Health:

Prescription Medications: Bring sufficient supplies of any prescription medications you may need.

Basic First Aid Kit: Include essentials like pain relievers, bandaids, and any personal medications.

Documents and Essentials:

Passport and Visa: Ensure your passport is valid for at least six months beyond your planned departure date. Carry a printed copy of your visa.

Travel Insurance: Carry a copy of your travel insurance policy and emergency contact details.

Local Currency: Have some local currency in cash for small purchases and transportation.

Travel Wallet: Keep your essential documents organized in a secure travel wallet.

Miscellaneous Items:

Reusable Water Bottle: Stay hydrated, especially in the warmer months.

Backpack or Day Bag: Useful for day trips and carrying essentials.

Tissues or Wet Wipes: Handy for freshening up during the day.

Cultural Considerations:

Respectful Attire: While casual clothing is generally acceptable, pack slightly more formal attire for upscale dining or events.

No Public Displays of Affection: Respect local customs by avoiding public displays of affection.

Evening Wear:

Casual and Formal Options: Dubai has a vibrant nightlife, so pack both casual and slightly more formal attire for evenings out.

Weather-Appropriate Accessories:

Light Jacket or Sweater: Evenings in winter can be cooler, so bring a light jacket or sweater.

Remember to check the weather forecast closer to your travel dates for any unexpected changes.

By packing smartly and considering cultural sensitivities, you'll be well-prepared for a comfortable and enjoyable stay in Dubai.

Souvenirs to purchase in Dubai

Dubai offers a plethora of unique and culturally rich souvenirs that can serve as cherished mementos of your visit. Here are some popular souvenirs to consider, along with a general price range:

Arabian Carpets and Rugs:

Description: Handwoven carpets and rugs with intricate designs and vibrant colors.

Price Range: Prices vary based on size, quality, and intricacy. Small rugs can start from around 200 AED, while larger, more intricate pieces can go into the thousands.

Arabic Perfumes (Oud and Attar):

Description: Fragrances derived from agarwood (oud) or essential oils (attar), offering a rich and unique scent.

Price Range: Small bottles can start from around 100 AED, while more exclusive blends can be significantly higher.

Gold and Jewelry:

Description: Dubai is renowned for its gold souks, offering a wide array of gold and jewelry items.

Price Range: Prices vary based on the weight of the gold and the intricacy of the design.

Small gold items or gold-plated jewelry can start from 200 AED, while more elaborate pieces can go into the thousands.

Camel Milk Chocolate:

Description: Chocolate made with camel milk, a unique and locally produced treat.

Price Range: Boxes of camel milk chocolates typically range from 30 AED to 100 AED.

Arabic Coffee Pots (Dallah):

Description: Traditional Arabic coffee pots made from brass or other metals, often adorned with intricate designs.

Price Range: Depending on size and materials, Dallahs can range from 100 AED to several hundred AED.

Arabic Tea Sets:

Description: Elegant tea sets featuring traditional Arabic designs, perfect for serving tea or coffee.

Price Range: Quality sets can start from around 200 AED and go up based on materials and craftsmanship.

Traditional Clothing (Abaya and Kandura):

Description: Traditional garments like the abaya for women and kandura for men, often beautifully embellished.

Price Range: Prices vary based on the quality of fabric and embellishments. Simple abayas or kanduras can start from around 100 AED, while more intricate designs can be higher.

Arabic Calligraphy Art:

Description: Artistic pieces featuring Arabic calligraphy, often depicting verses from the Quran or traditional sayings.

Price Range: Prices can vary significantly based on size, framing, and the artist. Small pieces can start from 50 AED, while larger and more detailed artworks can go into the hundreds or even thousands.

Dates and Date Products:

Description: Locally grown dates and date-based products, such as date chocolates and date syrup.

Price Range: Prices for date products can range from 20 AED to 100 AED or more, depending on the type and packaging.

Arabic Lanterns (Fanous):

Description: Ornate lanterns that add a touch of Arabian charm to any space.

Price Range: Prices vary based on size, materials, and intricacy. Small lanterns can start from around 50 AED, while larger or more elaborate ones can be higher.

Prices mentioned are approximate and can vary based on factors like location, quality, and the specific store.

It's advisable to explore different markets and shops to find the best deals on these unique Dubai souvenirs.

Getting to Dubai- Airports and Airlines

Getting to Dubai is a seamless process, thanks to its well-connected international airports and a multitude of reputable airlines. Here's a comprehensive guide to help you plan your journey:

Airports:

Dubai International Airport (DXB):

Description: Dubai International Airport, located in the Al Garhoud district, is the primary international airport serving Dubai.

Facilities: DXB offers a wide range of facilities, including lounges, shopping, dining, and transportation options.

Terminals: The airport has three terminals - Terminal 1, Terminal 2, and Terminal 3. Terminal 3 is the main hub for Emirates Airlines.

Al Maktoum International Airport (DWC):

Description: Also known as Dubai World Central, DWC is another international airport in Dubai.

Use: DWC mainly handles cargo flights and some passenger flights. It is gradually expanding its passenger services.

Airlines:

Emirates Airlines:

Hub: Dubai's flagship carrier, Emirates, operates from Dubai International Airport

(DXB) and is one of the largest and most renowned airlines globally.

Destinations: Emirates connects Dubai to numerous destinations worldwide, providing excellent in-flight services and a vast network.

Flydubai:

Hub: Flydubai is a low-cost airline based at Dubai International Airport (DXB).

Destinations: Flydubai offers affordable flights to various destinations, particularly in the Middle East, Africa, Europe, and Asia.

Etihad Airways:

Location: While Etihad is based in Abu Dhabi, the capital of the UAE, it operates flights to and from Dubai International Airport.

Destinations: Etihad serves a global network, providing convenient options for travelers.

Other Major Airlines:

Dubai is a major global hub, and many other international airlines operate flights to and from the city, including but not limited to Qatar Airways, British Airways, Lufthansa, and more.

Travel Tips:

Book Flights in Advance:

To secure the best fares, it's advisable to book your flights well in advance.

Transfers Between Airports:

If your flight arrives at Al Maktoum International Airport (DWC) and you need to transfer to Dubai International Airport (DXB) or vice versa, plan for transportation options, such as taxis or airport shuttles.

Visa Requirements:

Check visa requirements well in advance and ensure you have the necessary documents for entry into Dubai.

Airport Facilities:

Both DXB and DWC offer a wide range of amenities, including duty-free shopping, lounges, currency exchange, and dining options.

Transportation from the Airport:

Taxis, ride-sharing services, and hotel shuttles are readily available for transportation from the airports to various parts of the city.

Always check for any travel restrictions, visa requirements, and the latest information on flight schedules before planning your trip to Dubai.

With its world-class airports and a multitude of airlines, Dubai ensures a smooth and comfortable journey for travelers from around the globe.

Transportation within Dubai

Dubai boasts a well-developed and efficient transportation system that makes navigating the city convenient for both residents and visitors. Here's a comprehensive guide to transportation within Dubai:

Metro:

Description: The Dubai Metro is a driverless, fully automated metro network that connects key areas of the city.

Lines: The metro system has two lines - the Red Line and the Green Line.

Stations: Major stations include those near popular attractions like Burj Khalifa, Dubai Mall, and Dubai Marina.

Buses:

Description: The Roads and Transport Authority (RTA) operates an extensive bus network in Dubai, connecting various neighborhoods and key landmarks.

Types of Buses: Dubai has standard city buses, express buses, and intercity buses serving different routes.

Payment: Bus fares can be paid using the Nol Card, which is a smart card used for various public transportation modes.

Taxis:

Description: Taxis are widely available and offer a convenient mode of transportation.

Taxi Types: Dubai has regular taxis, which are cream-colored, and luxury taxis, which are silver. Both can be hailed on the street or booked through RTA's taxi booking service.

Payment: Taxis accept cash and credit cards, and fares are metered.

Dubai Tram:

Description: The Dubai Tram runs along a track parallel to the Dubai Marina and Jumeirah Beach Residence.

Connectivity: It connects with the Dubai Metro at certain stations, providing an integrated transportation experience.

Water Taxis and Abras:

Description: Traditional wooden boats known as abras operate on Dubai Creek, providing a scenic and economical means of crossing the water.

Water Taxis: Water taxis, also known as water limousines, offer private transportation across Dubai's waterways.

Ride-Sharing Services:

Description: Services like Uber and local alternative Careem operate in Dubai, offering an additional option for convenient point-to-point transportation.

Payment: Payment is usually done through the app, and both cash and card options are available.

Rental Cars:

Description: Car rental companies operate in Dubai, providing flexibility for travelers who prefer to drive.

Driving: Dubai has well-maintained roads and an organized traffic system. However, be aware of local traffic rules and conditions.

Bicycle Rentals:

Description: Some areas in Dubai offer bicycle rental services, promoting a healthier and eco-friendly means of transportation.

Monorail:

Description: The Palm Jumeirah Monorail connects the Palm Jumeirah to the mainland, offering a scenic route with views of the iconic Palm.

Electric Scooters:

Description: Electric scooters are available for short-distance travel in certain areas. Users can rent them using smartphone apps.

Travel Tips:

Nol Card: Consider getting a Nol Card, a smart card that can be used across various public transportation modes, including the metro, buses, and water transport.

Peak Hours: Be mindful of peak traffic hours, especially during morning and evening rush hours.

Dubai's diverse transportation options cater to different preferences and travel needs, making it easy for visitors to explore the city efficiently and comfortably.

Accommodation- Hotel Options

Dubai offers a vast array of accommodation options, ranging from luxurious hotels with world-class amenities to budget-friendly alternatives. Here's a guide to various hotel options in Dubai across different price ranges:

Luxury Hotels:

Burj Al Arab Jumeirah:

Description: Often regarded as one of the most luxurious hotels globally, Burj Al Arab Jumeirah is an iconic sail-shaped structure. It offers opulent suites, private butler service, and exquisite dining options.

Price Range: (Prices start from around 2,000 AED per night).

Armani Hotel Dubai:

Description: Located in the Burj Khalifa, the Armani Hotel offers chic and sophisticated accommodations designed by Giorgio Armani.

Guests enjoy exclusive access to the Burj Khalifa and Dubai Mall.

Price Range: $$$$ (Prices start from around 1,500 AED per night).

Mid-Range Hotels:

Rove Downtown:

Description: A trendy and modern hotel located in Downtown Dubai, offering comfortable rooms, a pool, and a convenient location near major attractions.

Price Range: (Prices start from around 400 AED per night).

Holiday Inn Express Dubai Jumeirah:

Description: A reliable and budget-friendly option, this hotel in Jumeirah offers comfortable rooms, complimentary breakfast, and easy access to public transport.

Price Range: (Prices start from around 300 AED per night).

Budget-Friendly Stays:

Zabeel House Mini by Jumeirah:

Description: This budget-friendly option offers stylish rooms and a vibrant atmosphere. It's located in the Al Seef area, close to Dubai Creek.

Price Range: (Prices start from around 200 AED per night).

Rove City Centre:

Description: Situated near Deira City Centre, Rove City Centre provides modern accommodations with a focus on affordability and convenience.

Price Range: (Prices start from around 250 AED per night).

Boutique Hotels:

La Ville Hotel & Suites CITY WALK, Dubai, Autograph Collection:

Description: A boutique hotel located in the trendy CITY WALK district, offering a blend of modern luxury and personalized service.

Price Range: (Prices start from around 600 AED per night).

XVA Art Hotel:

Description: Nestled in the historic Al Fahidi neighborhood, this boutique hotel features unique rooms adorned with contemporary art, creating a cultural and artistic ambiance.

Price Range: (Prices start from around 400 AED per night).

Family-Friendly Options:

Atlantis The Palm:

Description: A family-friendly resort located on the Palm Jumeirah, Atlantis offers a water park, aquarium, and various entertainment options for all ages.

Price Range: (Prices start from around 1,000 AED per night).

Jumeirah Beach Hotel:

Description: Overlooking the Arabian Gulf, this hotel features family-friendly amenities, including a Kids' Club, water sports, and a private beach.

Price Range: (Prices start from around 800 AED per night).

Unique Accommodations:

Al Maha, a Luxury Collection Desert Resort & Spa:

Description: Located in the desert conservation reserve, Al Maha offers luxurious Bedouin-style suites with private pools, providing a unique desert experience.

Price Range: (Prices start from around 4,000 AED per night).

QE2 - Queen Elizabeth 2:

Description: A floating hotel on the historic Queen Elizabeth 2 cruise ship, offering a blend of maritime history and modern comfort.

Price Range: (Prices start from around 600 AED per night).

Remember that prices can vary based on factors such as the time of booking, season, and room availability.

It's recommended to book in advance, especially during peak tourist seasons, to secure the best rates.

The Palm Jumeirah

History:

The Palm Jumeirah, an engineering marvel in the heart of Dubai, is an artificial archipelago designed in the shape of a palm tree. Construction on this iconic project began in 2001 and was completed in 2006.

The idea behind the Palm Jumeirah was to extend Dubai's coastline and create a luxurious residential, leisure, and entertainment destination on the Arabian Gulf.

Location:

Situated off the coast of Dubai, the Palm Jumeirah is easily accessible from the mainland. It is located in the northern part of the city, adjacent to the Dubai Marina. The Palm is connected to the mainland by a monorail and a bridge.

Key Features:

Fronds and Crescent:

The Palm Jumeirah comprises a trunk, 17 fronds, and a surrounding crescent. The trunk serves as the main transportation spine, while the fronds and crescent host a mix of residential villas, apartments, and high-end resorts.

Atlantis, The Palm:

One of the Palm's most iconic landmarks is Atlantis, The Palm, a luxurious resort located at the apex of the crescent. This world-class hotel features stunning architecture, marine attractions, and a water park.

Luxury Residences:

The Palm offers some of the most exclusive and opulent residential properties in Dubai, ranging from lavish villas on the fronds to high-rise apartments along the trunk.

Aquaventure Waterpark:

Atlantis, The Palm is home to the Aquaventure Waterpark, a thrilling attraction with water slides, river rides, and encounters with marine life.

It's a perfect destination for families and adventure seekers.

The Pointe:

The Pointe is a vibrant waterfront dining and entertainment destination located at the tip of the Palm's trunk. It features a variety of restaurants, shops, and a state-of-the-art fountain show.

Monorail:

The Palm Jumeirah is connected to the mainland by a monorail system. This provides residents and visitors with a unique perspective of the palm-shaped island and its stunning surroundings.

Beaches and Resorts:

The crescent of the Palm boasts pristine beaches and high-end resorts, offering an idyllic setting for relaxation and indulgence.

Nakheel Mall:

Nakheel Mall, situated at the base of the trunk, is a premium shopping and dining destination. It features a wide array of international brands and culinary delights.

Tourist Attractions:

Palm Jumeirah Boardwalk:

Take a stroll along the Palm Jumeirah Boardwalk for breathtaking views of the Dubai skyline, the Arabian Gulf, and the Atlantis resort.

Helicopter Tours:

For a truly spectacular view of the Palm Jumeirah, consider taking a helicopter tour, offering an aerial perspective of this architectural wonder.

Fine Dining:

The Palm hosts an array of fine-dining restaurants, many with panoramic views of the sea and the city. Indulge in a culinary experience while enjoying the luxury surroundings.

Travel Tips:

Timing: Visit the Palm Jumeirah in the evening to witness the stunning sunset and the city lights.

Transportation: Utilize the monorail, taxis, or ride-sharing services for convenient transportation around the Palm.

Reservations: For popular attractions and dining spots, consider making reservations in advance, especially during peak tourist seasons.

The Palm Jumeirah stands as a testament to Dubai's ambition and innovation.

Its luxurious offerings, stunning architecture, and vibrant atmosphere make it a must-visit destination for tourists seeking an unforgettable experience in the city of dreams.

Dubai Marina

History:

Dubai Marina, a man-made canal city, is a symbol of contemporary luxury and urban design. Construction on this iconic waterfront development began in 2003 and was completed in 2008.

The inspiration behind Dubai Marina was to create an upscale, cosmopolitan environment with a mix of residential, commercial, and leisure spaces along the picturesque Arabian Gulf.

Location:

Nestled along the shoreline of the Arabian Gulf, Dubai Marina is strategically located in the heart of "New Dubai." It is situated between the Jebel Ali Port and the area known as the Dubai Internet City. The Marina is easily accessible from Sheikh Zayed Road and is in close proximity to other key attractions like Jumeirah Beach Residence (JBR) and Palm Jumeirah.

Key Features:

Man-Made Canal:

At the heart of Dubai Marina is a two-mile-long artificial canal, meticulously carved into the city's landscape.

This waterway connects the entire district, offering residents and visitors stunning waterfront views.

Skyline of Towers:

Dubai Marina is renowned for its iconic skyline dominated by sleek, high-rise residential towers, each vying for attention with unique architectural designs.

The nighttime illumination of these structures creates a captivating spectacle.

The Walk at JBR:

Adjacent to Dubai Marina is The Walk at JBR, a bustling promenade featuring shops, restaurants, and cafes. It's a vibrant destination for shopping, dining, and enjoying the lively atmosphere.

Dubai Marina Mall:

Dubai Marina Mall, situated at the center of the district, is a shopping and entertainment hub with a diverse range of retail outlets, dining options, and a cinema complex.

Marina Yacht Club:

The Dubai Marina Yacht Club is a haven for yacht enthusiasts. It offers berthing facilities, marine services, and is surrounded by upscale restaurants with marina views.

Luxury Residences:

Dubai Marina hosts a mix of luxury apartments and penthouses, providing residents with panoramic views of the Gulf and the city. The properties along the waterfront are especially coveted.

Dubai Marina Walk:

The Dubai Marina Walk is a picturesque pedestrian pathway that runs along the canal, offering a serene environment for jogging, cycling, or simply enjoying a leisurely stroll.

Tourist Attractions:

Boat Tours and Cruises:

Explore Dubai Marina from the water by taking a boat tour or dinner cruise. These excursions provide a unique perspective of the skyline and waterfront.

Skydive Dubai:

For the adrenaline junkies, Skydive Dubai offers an exhilarating experience, allowing you to skydive over the iconic Dubai Marina skyline.

Public Beaches:

The public beaches near Dubai Marina, such as JBR Beach, offer pristine sands and the inviting waters of the Arabian Gulf. Ideal for sunbathing, swimming, and water sports.

Travel Tips:

Sunset Views: Visit Dubai Marina during the evening to witness a stunning sunset over the Arabian Gulf.

Water Taxis: Consider taking a water taxi to navigate the canal and enjoy the scenic beauty of Dubai Marina.

Dining by the Water: Many restaurants along the canal offer outdoor seating with picturesque views, making it a perfect spot for a leisurely meal.

Dubai Marina is a testament to Dubai's commitment to modernity and innovation. Its combination of architectural marvels, waterfront living, and vibrant lifestyle make it a captivating destination for tourists seeking a blend of luxury and coastal charm in the heart of the city.

Jumeirah Beach Residence (JBR)

History:

Jumeirah Beach Residence, commonly known as JBR, is a vibrant waterfront community that has transformed the coastline of Dubai.

Development on JBR began in 2002, with the goal of creating a bustling urban beach destination that seamlessly combines residential living with retail, dining, and entertainment options.

Completed in 2010, JBR has since become one of Dubai's most sought-after neighborhoods.

Location:

Located along the Arabian Gulf in the Dubai Marina district, JBR stretches across 1.7 kilometers of pristine shoreline.

The strategic location provides residents and visitors with stunning views of the sea, the Dubai Marina skyline, and the iconic Ain Dubai (Dubai Eye) Ferris wheel on Bluewaters Island.

Key Features:

The Beach at JBR:

Central to the JBR experience is "The Beach," a vibrant outdoor destination featuring a pedestrian-friendly promenade lined with shops, restaurants, cafes, and entertainment options.

Residential Towers:

JBR is characterized by an impressive array of residential towers, offering a mix of apartments, penthouses, and luxury living spaces. Residents enjoy direct access to the beach and a variety of amenities.

Ain Dubai (Dubai Eye):

Dominating the JBR skyline is Ain Dubai, the world's largest and tallest observation wheel. Situated on Bluewaters Island, Ain Dubai offers breathtaking views of JBR, the Dubai Marina, and the city beyond.

Outdoor Activities:

JBR's seaside location invites outdoor enthusiasts to engage in various activities, including jogging, cycling, and water sports.

The public beaches offer ample space for relaxation and recreation.

Retail and Dining:

The Walk at JBR is a bustling boulevard filled with an eclectic mix of shops, boutiques, cafes, and restaurants. It's a popular destination for both residents and tourists looking for a leisurely shopping and dining experience.

Street Art and Murals:

JBR is adorned with vibrant street art and murals, adding an artistic and colorful touch to the urban landscape. These art installations contribute to the dynamic atmosphere of the neighborhood.

Tourist Attractions:

The Beachfront:

Enjoy the sun, sea, and sand at JBR's public beaches. The Beachfront area offers opportunities for water sports, sunbathing, and family-friendly activities.

The Walk at JBR:

Explore The Walk, where you can shop for fashion, accessories, and souvenirs, or dine at an array of international restaurants offering diverse culinary delights.

Ain Dubai Experience:

Take a trip to Bluewaters Island to experience Ain Dubai, where you can ride the observation wheel for panoramic views of JBR and the Dubai skyline.

Travel Tips:

Visit in the Evening: JBR comes alive in the evening with a vibrant atmosphere, illuminated structures, and a variety of entertainment options.

Waterfront Dining: Many restaurants along The Walk and The Beach offer outdoor seating with views of the sea, making it a perfect spot for a seaside meal.

Weekend Events: Check for events and activities happening during the weekends, such as markets, street performances, and cultural events.

Jumeirah Beach Residence embodies the dynamic spirit of Dubai's coastal lifestyle. Whether you seek relaxation on the beach, trendy shopping, or a diverse culinary experience, JBR promises an unforgettable blend of leisure and entertainment along the stunning Arabian Gulf.

Burj Khalifa

History:

Burj Khalifa, the iconic skyscraper that defines Dubai's skyline, is a symbol of architectural prowess and modern innovation.

Construction on this monumental structure began in 2004 and was completed in 2010, officially opening to the public on January 4, 2010.

The vision behind Burj Khalifa was to create an extraordinary landmark that would not only break records in height but also redefine the boundaries of design and engineering.

Location:

Situated in the heart of Downtown Dubai, Burj Khalifa is centrally located near key attractions such as The Dubai Mall, The Dubai Fountain, and Dubai Opera.

Its strategic position within the city's most dynamic district makes it easily accessible and a focal point for tourists and residents alike.

Key Features:

Record-Breaking Height:

Burj Khalifa holds the title of the world's tallest building, soaring to a height of 828 meters (2,717 feet). The tower's design draws inspiration from Islamic architecture, with a series of setbacks and a spire at its pinnacle.

Observation Decks:

At the Top, Burj Khalifa's observation decks, offer mesmerizing panoramic views of the city, the Arabian Gulf, and the surrounding desert.

The experience provides a glimpse into Dubai's transformation from a desert landscape to a thriving metropolis.

Atmosphere Restaurant:

Located on the 122nd floor, At.mosphere is one of the world's highest restaurants. Visitors can indulge in fine dining while enjoying unparalleled views of the city below.

Luxury Residences:

Burj Khalifa is not only a commercial and tourism hub but also home to exclusive residential apartments, offering an elite living experience with unparalleled amenities and services.

Armani Hotel Dubai:

The Armani Hotel, located within Burj Khalifa, reflects the luxurious lifestyle the tower embodies. Designed by fashion legend Giorgio Armani, the hotel offers unparalleled elegance and sophistication.

Sky Lobbies:

The tower features sky lobbies at various intervals, providing residents and visitors with unique spaces for relaxation, socializing, and enjoying breathtaking views.

Tourist Attractions:

At the Top, Burj Khalifa:

Visit the observation decks on the 148th, 125th, and 124th floors for a bird's-eye view of Dubai. Time your visit to catch the stunning sunset or witness the city lights come to life in the evening.

The Dubai Fountain:

Adjacent to Burj Khalifa is The Dubai Fountain, one of the world's largest dancing fountains. The fountain's synchronized water and light shows, set against the backdrop of the tower, are a captivating spectacle.

Dubai Mall:

Connected to Burj Khalifa is The Dubai Mall, a shopping and entertainment extravaganza that features over 1,200 shops, various dining options, and attractions such as the Dubai Aquarium and Underwater Zoo.

Travel Tips:

Book Tickets in Advance: To avoid long queues, especially during peak hours, it's advisable to book tickets for At the Top, Burj Khalifa in advance.

Sunset Visits: Plan your visit during sunset for a magical experience as the city transitions from day to night.

Combine Experiences: Combine your visit to Burj Khalifa with nearby attractions like

The Dubai Fountain show or a shopping spree at The Dubai Mall.

Burj Khalifa stands not only as a towering marvel but as a testament to Dubai's ambition, vision, and commitment to pushing the boundaries of architectural excellence.

A visit to this iconic structure is an essential part of experiencing the dynamic and ever-evolving city of Dubai.

The Dubai Mall

History:

The Dubai Mall, inaugurated on November 4, 2008, is a testament to Dubai's commitment to grandeur and excellence.

As one of the largest shopping and entertainment destinations globally, The Dubai Mall has evolved into a city within a city, offering a diverse array of experiences beyond traditional retail.

Its construction was part of the visionary plan to transform Dubai into a global shopping and tourism hub.

Location:

Nestled in the heart of Downtown Dubai, The Dubai Mall is strategically positioned at the base of the iconic Burj Khalifa. Its central location makes it easily accessible from various parts of the city, attracting millions of visitors annually.

Key Features:

Sheer Size and Scale:

Covering an impressive area of over 13 million square feet, The Dubai Mall is not just a shopping destination but a sprawling complex that houses an extensive array of retail outlets, dining establishments, and entertainment facilities.

Fashion Avenue:

For luxury shoppers, Fashion Avenue is a dedicated precinct within The Dubai Mall featuring high-end designer boutiques, luxury brands, and flagship stores.

The Souk:

Inspired by traditional Arabian markets, The Souk offers a unique shopping experience with a diverse range of stores selling jewelry, traditional artifacts, and souvenirs.

Entertainment and Attractions:

The Dubai Mall is home to a variety of attractions, including the Dubai Aquarium and Underwater Zoo, KidZania, an Olympic-sized ice rink, and the VR Park, offering cutting-edge virtual reality experiences.

Dining and Culinary Delights:

From casual eateries to fine-dining restaurants, The Dubai Mall boasts a wide range of dining options catering to diverse palates. Visitors can enjoy meals with views of the Burj Khalifa or dine in the themed restaurants.

Dubai Fountain Views:

The Dubai Fountain, one of the world's largest choreographed fountains, is located right outside The Dubai Mall. Visitors can witness the captivating fountain shows set against the backdrop of the Burj Khalifa.

The Waterfall:

A centerpiece of The Dubai Mall is the Waterfall, a mesmerizing art installation that cascades through all four levels of the mall.

The Waterfall adds a touch of nature and artistry to the shopping experience.

Tourist Attractions:

Dubai Aquarium and Underwater Zoo:

Home to thousands of aquatic animals, the Dubai Aquarium and Underwater Zoo provide an immersive experience for visitors. The highlight is the walkthrough tunnel, allowing guests to be surrounded by marine life.

KidZania:

KidZania is an interactive educational and entertainment center for children, offering them the chance to role-play various professions in a mini city environment.

Dubai Ice Rink:

The Olympic-sized Dubai Ice Rink is a popular attraction for ice-skating enthusiasts. It caters to all skill levels and hosts various events and activities.

Travel Tips:

Plan Ahead: Given the sheer size of The Dubai Mall, it's advisable to plan your visit and prioritize the attractions and stores you wish to explore.

Family-Friendly: The Dubai Mall is family-friendly, with dedicated areas for children's entertainment and play.

Visit During Fountain Shows: Time your visit to coincide with the spectacular Dubai Fountain shows in the evenings.

The Dubai Mall is not merely a shopping destination; it's an immersive experience that captures the essence of Dubai's commitment to luxury, entertainment, and innovation.

A visit to this retail haven is a must for tourists seeking a taste of the city's vibrant and cosmopolitan lifestyle.

Dubai Fountain Show

History:

The Dubai Fountain, inaugurated in 2009, is a captivating aquatic spectacle located at the base of the iconic Burj Khalifa and adjacent to The Dubai Mall.

This innovative fountain was designed by the same team behind the Bellagio Fountains in Las Vegas, USA.

Its creation marked a significant addition to Dubai's impressive lineup of architectural wonders and entertainment offerings.

Location:

Situated on the 30-acre Burj Khalifa Lake, the Dubai Fountain is at the heart of

Downtown Dubai, providing a stunning backdrop to the Burj Khalifa and overlooking The Dubai Mall.

Its strategic location ensures that both residents and tourists can easily witness its mesmerizing performances.

Key Features:

World's Largest Choreographed Fountain System:

The Dubai Fountain holds the distinction of being the world's largest choreographed fountain system.

It spans over 900 feet in length and shoots water jets as high as 500 feet into the air, creating a spectacle that is visible from various vantage points.

Synchronized Water, Light, and Sound:

What makes the Dubai Fountain truly unique is its synchronization of water jets, illuminated by 6,600 lights, and choreographed to dance in harmony with a diverse range of music genres, including classical, contemporary, and Arabic music.

Evening Performances:

The Dubai Fountain performs daily, with evening shows beginning after sunset. The illuminated water jets are further enhanced by the city lights, creating a magical ambiance.

Variety of Performances:

The fountain showcases a variety of performances throughout the day, with each show lasting about 5 minutes. The choreography is constantly evolving, and visitors can experience different musical and visual experiences during their visit.

Dubai Fountain Lake Ride:

For a unique perspective, visitors can embark on the Dubai Fountain Lake Ride, a boat tour that takes them up close to the fountain.

This immersive experience allows guests to feel the power and grandeur of the fountain's water jets.

Tourist Attractions:

Burj Khalifa Views:

The Dubai Fountain serves as a spectacular complement to the Burj Khalifa, and visitors can enjoy the fountain show against the backdrop of the world's tallest building.

The Dubai Mall:

The Dubai Fountain is conveniently located near The Dubai Mall, offering visitors the opportunity to combine their fountain experience with shopping, dining, and entertainment at one of the world's largest malls.

Observation Decks:

The observation decks of the Burj Khalifa, such as At the Top, provide panoramic views of the Dubai Fountain and its performances. It's a fantastic way to witness the show from an elevated perspective.

Travel Tips:

Arrive Early: Secure a good viewing spot by arriving a bit early, especially during peak hours, to ensure a prime position for the show.

Visit at Night: The evening shows, when the fountain is illuminated, are particularly enchanting. Combine your visit with the spectacle of city lights.

The Dubai Fountain Show is a dazzling testament to Dubai's commitment to providing a multisensory experience for residents and visitors alike.

Whether viewed from the shores of Burj Khalifa Lake, a nearby rooftop, or even from the decks of the Burj Khalifa, the fountain's performances are a must-see for anyone seeking a taste of Dubai's magic and innovation.

Dubai Creek

History:

Dubai Creek, also known as Khor Dubai, has been at the heart of Dubai's history and development.

This natural saltwater inlet played a crucial role in the early days of the city, serving as a trading port for dhows and facilitating commerce with neighboring regions.

The creek has witnessed Dubai's transformation from a modest fishing and trading village to a global metropolis.

Location:

Stretching approximately 14 kilometers, Dubai Creek divides the city into two main sections: Deira on the northern bank and Bur Dubai to the south. The creek flows into the Arabian Gulf, providing a natural waterway that has been a lifeline for the city's economic activities.

Key Features:

Traditional Dhows:

Dubai Creek is adorned with traditional wooden dhows, showcasing the city's maritime heritage.

These boats were historically used for trading and transporting goods, and today, they offer tourists scenic cruises along the creek.

Al Fahidi Historic District:

On the Bur Dubai side of the creek lies Al Fahidi Historic District, a charming area characterized by narrow winding streets, wind-tower architecture, and restored historical buildings that house museums, art galleries, and cultural institutions.

Gold and Spice Souks:

Deira, on the northern bank, is home to vibrant traditional markets known as souks.

The Gold Souk and Spice Souk attract visitors with their bustling atmosphere and a dazzling array of precious metals, gemstones, and aromatic spices.

Dhow Wharfage:

The Dhow Wharfage along the creek's shores in Deira is a hub of activity where dhows are loaded and unloaded with goods destined for various markets. It offers a glimpse into the traditional trading practices that have persisted for centuries.

Dubai Creek Park:

Dubai Creek Park is a sprawling green space along the creek, providing a recreational area for families and offering stunning views of the city's skyline. The park features walking trails, playgrounds, and picnic areas.

Water Taxis and Abras:

Abras, traditional wooden water taxis, ferry passengers across the creek between Deira and Bur Dubai.

This affordable and authentic mode of transportation provides a unique perspective of the city.

Tourist Attractions:

Heritage and Diving Village:

Located in Al Shindagha area, the Heritage and Diving Village offers a glimpse into Dubai's maritime history and cultural heritage.

Visitors can explore traditional Emirati architecture, artifacts, and exhibits.

Dubai Creek Golf and Yacht Club:

Golf enthusiasts can enjoy a round of golf at the Dubai Creek Golf and Yacht Club, which boasts an 18-hole championship course along the creek.

Dubai Dolphinarium:

Families can visit the Dubai Dolphinarium near the creek to enjoy live dolphin and seal shows, adding a touch of entertainment to their Dubai Creek experience.

Travel Tips:

Creek Cruises: Consider taking a traditional abra or dhow cruise along the creek to appreciate the cityscape from the water.

Evening Strolls: Enjoy a leisurely evening stroll along the Al Seef promenade, which combines modern amenities with a traditional ambience.

Visit the Souks: Explore the Gold and Spice Souks in Deira for a sensory experience filled with vibrant colors, scents, and bustling market activity.

Dubai Creek remains a testament to Dubai's rich history and the harmonious blend of tradition and modernity. Whether you're interested in exploring cultural heritage, experiencing traditional markets, or enjoying a scenic cruise, Dubai Creek provides a unique and multifaceted perspective of the city.

Miracle Garden

History:

Dubai Miracle Garden, opened in 2013, is a horticultural marvel situated in the heart of the Arabian desert.

What was once a barren landscape has been transformed into a breathtaking floral oasis, showcasing the creativity, innovation, and commitment to beauty that Dubai is renowned for.

The garden is a testament to the city's dedication to turning ambitious dreams into reality.

Location:

Located in Dubailand, Dubai Miracle Garden is easily accessible from the city center. Its strategic location near the Arabian Ranches and the Dubai Autodrome makes it a popular destination for both residents and tourists seeking a burst of color in the desert.

Key Features:

World's Largest Flower Garden:

Dubai Miracle Garden holds the Guinness World Record for the world's largest flower garden.

The garden spans over 72,000 square meters and features an ever-evolving display of vibrant flowers arranged in intricate patterns and designs.

Breathtaking Floral Displays:

The garden is a riot of colors with over 150 million flowers of various species.

Visitors can witness a kaleidoscope of blooms, including petunias, marigolds, roses, and a variety of exotic flowers, meticulously arranged to form arches, heart-shaped pathways, and themed structures.

Heart Passage:

One of the iconic features is the Heart Passage, a heart-shaped pathway adorned with an abundance of flowers.

It's a popular spot for visitors seeking romantic and picturesque photo opportunities.

Butterfly Garden:

Within the Miracle Garden, there is a dedicated Butterfly Garden where visitors can marvel at the beauty of butterflies amidst a lush, flower-filled environment.

Aromatic Garden:

The Aromatic Garden engages the senses with fragrant blooms, creating a sensory experience that complements the visual beauty of the floral displays.

Themed Gardens:

The garden is divided into themed areas, each with its own unique displays. From the Umbrella Passage to the Disney Avenue, visitors can explore a variety of creative and whimsical arrangements.

Tourist Attractions:

Dubai Butterfly Garden:

Adjacent to Miracle Garden, the Dubai Butterfly Garden is home to thousands of butterflies representing different species. It's a tranquil and enchanting experience for nature enthusiasts.

Global Village:

During the winter months, visitors can combine their trip to Miracle Garden with a visit to the nearby Global Village, a multicultural festival park offering shopping, dining, and entertainment from around the world.

Travel Tips:

Best Time to Visit: The garden is open from November to April, with the blooming season at its peak during the cooler months.

Evening Stroll: Consider visiting in the late afternoon or evening to experience the garden illuminated by a magical play of lights.

Comfortable Attire: Wear comfortable clothing and bring sunscreen, as the desert sun can be intense.

Dubai Miracle Garden is a testament to Dubai's ability to turn dreams into reality, transforming a seemingly inhospitable environment into a lush, vibrant haven.

For tourists, it offers a unique and awe-inspiring experience that showcases the city's dedication to beauty, innovation, and the boundless possibilities of creativity in the desert landscape.

Museum of the Future

History:

Envisioned as a groundbreaking project, the Museum of the Future in Dubai represents the city's commitment to innovation, technology, and the exploration of possibilities.

While the museum's history is relatively short, its vision is rooted in Dubai's ambition to showcase cutting-edge advancements and ideas that will shape the future.

Location:

The Museum of the Future is strategically located near the iconic Burj Khalifa in Dubai's bustling financial district. Its position at the crossroads of innovation and tradition symbolizes Dubai's aspiration to be a global leader in technological and scientific progress.

Key Features (Anticipated):

Futuristic Architecture:

The museum is expected to be a marvel of architectural innovation, designed to embody the spirit of the future. Its unique and futuristic structure is likely to become an iconic landmark in Dubai's skyline.

Interactive Exhibits:

Anticipated to be a hub for technological exhibitions and interactive displays, the Museum of the Future aims to engage visitors with state-of-the-art exhibits that explore emerging technologies, artificial intelligence, robotics, sustainability, and more.

Innovation Hub:

As a center for innovation, the museum is expected to host conferences, workshops, and events that bring together experts, researchers, and innovators from various fields to collaborate on shaping the future.

Multimedia Installations:

Cutting-edge multimedia installations and immersive experiences are expected to be a focal point, providing visitors with a sensory journey into the possibilities of tomorrow.

Sustainability Initiatives:

Given Dubai's focus on sustainability, the museum is likely to incorporate eco-friendly features and showcase innovations in green technology and environmental conservation.

Anticipated Tourist Experience:

Tech-Savvy Exploration:

Visitors are likely to embark on a tech-savvy exploration, experiencing the latest advancements in virtual reality, augmented reality, and other immersive technologies.

Educational Opportunities:

The Museum of the Future is expected to offer educational programs, making it an informative destination for students, researchers, and technology enthusiasts keen on staying abreast of the latest breakthroughs.

Collaborative Events:

The museum may host collaborative events, bringing together leaders in various industries for discussions, presentations, and initiatives aimed at shaping a sustainable and innovative future.

Travel Tips (For Future Reference):

Check Opening Dates: Verify the museum's opening dates and any special events or exhibitions scheduled during your visit.

Plan Sufficient Time: Given the anticipated interactive nature of the exhibits, plan to spend sufficient time exploring the museum to fully appreciate its offerings.

As the Museum of the Future opens its doors, it is poised to become a symbol of Dubai's forward-thinking vision and commitment to pushing the boundaries of innovation. For tourists, it offers a glimpse into the possibilities that lie ahead, making it a must-visit destination for those intrigued by the intersection of technology, science, and imagination.

Sheikh Mohammed Centre for Cultural Understanding

History:

Founded in 1998, the Sheikh Mohammed Centre for Cultural Understanding (SMCCU) is a pioneering institution in Dubai dedicated to fostering cultural exchange and understanding.

Established under the vision of His Highness Sheikh Mohammed bin Rashid Al Maktoum, the ruler of Dubai, the center aims to bridge the gap between local Emiratis and visitors, fostering dialogue and appreciation for the rich cultural heritage of the United Arab Emirates.

Location:

The Sheikh Mohammed Centre for Cultural Understanding is located in the historic Al Fahidi District of Dubai, also known as Al Bastakiya.

This district is renowned for its well-preserved wind-tower architecture and traditional courtyard houses, providing a fitting backdrop for cultural exploration.

Key Features:

Cultural Breakfasts and Lunches:

One of the unique offerings of SMCCU is the opportunity for visitors to enjoy traditional Emirati meals with local hosts.

The "Cultural Breakfast" and "Cultural Lunch" sessions provide a platform for open conversations, allowing visitors to ask questions and gain insights into Emirati customs, traditions, and way of life.

Cultural Workshops:

SMCCU conducts interactive cultural workshops that cover various aspects of Emirati culture, including calligraphy, henna art, and traditional dress.

These hands-on experiences offer visitors the chance to immerse themselves in the cultural practices of the region.

Guided Heritage Tours:

The center organizes guided walking tours of the Al Fahidi Historic District, providing visitors with a glimpse into the history of Dubai and its transformation over the years. The tours explore the narrow lanes, museums, and historical landmarks of the district.

Jumeirah Mosque Tours:

SMCCU facilitates guided tours of the Jumeirah Mosque, one of the most iconic mosques in Dubai.

The tours aim to promote cross-cultural understanding by allowing visitors to learn about Islamic traditions and architecture.

Cultural Evenings:

Cultural evenings hosted by SMCCU offer visitors the chance to experience traditional Emirati music, dance, and cuisine in a relaxed and welcoming environment.

These events provide a festive atmosphere for cultural exchange.

Tourist Experience:

Open Dialogue: The SMCCU provides a platform for visitors to engage in open and respectful dialogue with Emirati hosts, encouraging the exchange of ideas and fostering cultural understanding.

Authentic Cultural Immersion: Through its programs and activities, SMCCU offers tourists an authentic and immersive experience of Emirati culture, allowing them to go beyond the surface and gain deeper insights.

Travel Tips:

Reservations: It is advisable to make reservations for cultural meals and workshops in advance, as these experiences can be in high demand.

Modest Attire: When visiting the Jumeirah Mosque or participating in cultural activities, it's respectful to dress modestly.

The Sheikh Mohammed Centre for Cultural Understanding stands as a beacon for cultural exchange and mutual respect in the heart of Dubai.

For tourists seeking a genuine and enlightening experience of Emirati culture, the center provides an invaluable opportunity to engage with locals, ask questions, and gain a deeper appreciation for the traditions that shape the identity of the United Arab Emirates.

Dubai Opera

History:

Dubai Opera, opened in 2016, is a cultural gem nestled in the heart of Downtown Dubai.

This architectural masterpiece was conceived as part of the city's vision to become a global cultural hub.

Designed to resemble the traditional Arabic dhow, Dubai Opera has swiftly become an iconic venue, hosting a diverse array of world-class performances and events.

Location:

Situated on the shores of the Burj Lake, Dubai Opera commands a prime location within the prestigious Downtown Dubai district. It is strategically positioned near other iconic landmarks, including Burj Khalifa, The Dubai Mall, and The Dubai Fountain, making it an integral part of the city's vibrant cultural and entertainment precinct.

Key Features:

Architectural Marvel:

The design of Dubai Opera pays homage to the traditional dhow, a symbol of Dubai's maritime heritage.

The sleek, contemporary structure features a retractable roof, allowing it to transform seamlessly from a state-of-the-art indoor venue to an open-air theater.

Versatile Performance Spaces:

Dubai Opera is a multifunctional venue with a capacity of over 2,000 seats. It hosts a variety of performances, including opera, ballet, classical concerts, theater productions, and contemporary performances.

The space is adaptable, accommodating different stage setups and configurations.

Acoustic Excellence:

Renowned for its exceptional acoustics, Dubai Opera provides an immersive and intimate experience for the audience.

The venue is equipped with cutting-edge technology to ensure that every note, spoken word, and movement on stage is delivered with precision and clarity.

Diverse Events and Performances:

Dubai Opera boasts a calendar filled with a diverse range of events, including performances by international artists, Broadway shows, classical concerts, comedy nights, and cultural festivals.

The venue is a cultural melting pot that caters to a broad spectrum of artistic tastes.

Opera Garden and Sky Garden:

The Opera Garden and Sky Garden offer stunning outdoor spaces with panoramic views of the cityscape.

These areas serve as pre-event gathering spaces, providing visitors with a scenic backdrop to complement their cultural experiences.

Tourist Experience:

World-Class Performances: Dubai Opera consistently attracts top-tier international performers, ensuring that visitors can witness world-class talent in an exquisite setting.

Cultural Immersion: The venue's diverse programming allows tourists to immerse themselves in a variety of cultural experiences, from classical music to contemporary performances.

Iconic Location: Dubai Opera's proximity to other iconic attractions makes it a convenient stop for tourists exploring the vibrant Downtown Dubai area.

Travel Tips:

Book Tickets in Advance: Given the popularity of events, it's advisable to book tickets well in advance, especially for high-demand performances.

Dress Code: While there is no strict dress code, many visitors choose to dress elegantly for their evening at Dubai Opera.

Dubai Opera stands as a symbol of Dubai's commitment to fostering a rich cultural scene.

With its striking design, world-class performances, and central location, it invites tourists to partake in a sophisticated and enchanting experience that seamlessly blends tradition with modernity.

Traditional Souks

Dubai's traditional souks, or markets, have been integral to the city's identity for centuries.

Rooted in the city's history as a trading hub, these vibrant marketplaces have evolved from humble beginnings to bustling centers of commerce.

The souks reflect Dubai's transition from a modest fishing and pearl-diving village to a global metropolis while retaining a deep connection to its cultural roots.

Location:

Located in the heart of Old Dubai, the traditional souks are scattered along the banks of Dubai Creek, specifically in the districts of Deira and Bur Dubai. Each souk has its unique charm and specializes in specific goods, creating a kaleidoscope of shopping experiences for visitors.

Key Features:

Gold Souk:

The Gold Souk in Deira is renowned worldwide for its dazzling display of gold and jewelry.

The market boasts an extensive array of gold ornaments, diamonds, and precious gems.

Visitors can witness the craftsmanship of skilled artisans and shop for exquisite pieces.

Spice Souk:

Adjacent to the Gold Souk, the Spice Souk is a sensory delight, with narrow lanes filled with the aromatic scents of spices, herbs, and traditional perfumes.

It's a journey into the world of fragrances and flavors, where visitors can purchase an array of spices unique to the region.

Textile Souk:

Nestled in the historic Bur Dubai area, the Textile Souk is a haven for fabric enthusiasts.

From vibrant silks to intricate lace and embroidered textiles, the market offers a rich assortment of materials. Tailors and dressmakers in the souk can create custom garments for visitors.

Perfume Souk:

Offering a blend of traditional and modern fragrances, the Perfume Souk in Deira allows visitors to explore a vast collection of perfumes, essential oils, and incense.

Perfume experts are on hand to guide customers in selecting scents that suit their preferences.

Souk Madinat Jumeirah:

While not as historic as the other souks, Souk Madinat Jumeirah is a recreation of a traditional Arabian market within the Madinat Jumeirah resort.

It combines the charm of a souk with modern amenities, offering a picturesque setting with waterways and stunning views of the Burj Al Arab.

Tourist Experience:

Cultural Exploration: The traditional souks provide an authentic glimpse into Dubai's cultural heritage, allowing tourists to witness age-old trading practices and engage with local vendors.

Bargaining: Bargaining is a common practice in the souks, and visitors have the opportunity to hone their negotiation skills while purchasing goods. Polite haggling is part of the cultural experience.

Local Cuisine: Surrounding the souks are eateries and cafes where tourists can indulge in local cuisine. From freshly squeezed fruit juices to traditional snacks, it's a culinary adventure for the taste buds.

Travel Tips:

Comfortable Attire: Wear comfortable clothing and footwear suitable for walking through narrow lanes and bustling markets.

Cash and Small Change: Some vendors may prefer cash, and having small change can make transactions smoother.

Respect Local Customs: Dress modestly, especially in more traditional areas, to respect local customs and traditions.

The traditional souks of Dubai are not just markets; they are living monuments to the city's history and heritage.

Tourists can immerse themselves in the vibrant tapestry of colors, scents, and sounds, experiencing the authentic charm of

Dubai's trading past while enjoying the diverse array of goods on offer.

IMG Worlds of Adventure

History:

IMG Worlds of Adventure, opened in 2016, stands as the world's largest indoor theme park, offering an immersive experience that combines entertainment, thrills, and beloved characters.

Developed by the Ilyas and Mustafa Galadari Group, this mega-attraction was conceived as part of Dubai's commitment to becoming a global hub for leisure and entertainment.

Location:

Situated in the heart of Dubai, IMG Worlds of Adventure is located on Sheikh Mohammed Bin Zayed Road, making it easily accessible from various parts of the city. Its central location and proximity to other attractions make it a key destination for families and thrill-seekers alike.

Key Features:

Indoor Theme Park:

IMG Worlds of Adventure is entirely indoors, providing a comfortable and climate-controlled environment.

This makes it an ideal year-round destination, escaping the extreme temperatures of the Dubai outdoors.

Marvel Zone:

One of the standout features is the Marvel Zone, featuring iconic Marvel Comics characters like Spider-Man, Iron Man, and the Hulk. Visitors can enjoy thrilling rides and attractions based on these beloved superheroes.

Cartoon Network Zone:

The park also hosts the Cartoon Network Zone, where characters from popular shows such as Adventure Time, The Powerpuff Girls, and Ben 10 come to life.

Attractions in this zone cater to a younger audience, offering a mix of fun and adventure.

Lost Valley - Dinosaur Adventure:

Adventure-seekers can explore the Lost Valley, a zone that brings prehistoric creatures back to life. With rides and attractions centered around dinosaurs, this area provides a unique blend of excitement and education.

IMG Boulevard and Novo Cinemas:

IMG Boulevard offers a variety of dining, shopping, and entertainment options. Additionally, Novo Cinemas within the park allows visitors to enjoy the latest blockbuster movies in a state-of-the-art cinema setting.

Haunted Hotel:

For those seeking a spine-chilling experience, the Haunted Hotel attraction promises a thrilling and immersive journey through a haunted mansion filled with surprises and scares.

Tourist Experience:

Multi-Generational Appeal:

IMG Worlds of Adventure caters to visitors of all ages, with a diverse range of attractions suitable for families, thrill-seekers, and those looking for a more relaxed experience.

Entertainment Beyond Rides:

In addition to rides, the park offers live entertainment, character meet-and-greets, and interactive experiences, enhancing the overall visitor experience.

Convenience and Accessibility:

The indoor setting makes the park accessible throughout the year, providing a convenient option for tourists regardless of weather conditions.

Travel Tips:

Fast Track Passes: Consider purchasing Fast Track passes to minimize wait times for popular rides during peak hours.

Plan for Full Day: Given the size and variety of attractions, plan to spend a full day at IMG Worlds of Adventure to make the most of the experience.

IMG Worlds of Adventure is a testament to Dubai's commitment to offering world-class entertainment and leisure options.

 Whether you're a fan of superheroes, cartoon characters, or dinosaur adventures, the park provides a thrilling and immersive escape into the realms of fantasy and fun.

Desert Safari Adventures for Families

History:

The Dubai Desert Safari has evolved from a traditional means of transportation and exploration in the desert to a popular tourist activity.

Historically, Bedouin nomads traversed the vast Arabian deserts using camels and established a symbiotic relationship with the arid landscape.

Today, the desert safari has become a cultural and recreational experience, allowing tourists to witness the beauty of the desert and partake in various activities.

Location:

Dubai Desert Safari experiences typically take place in the expansive deserts surrounding the city, with the most common being the Arabian Desert.

The proximity of the desert to the city allows for convenient access, making it a popular excursion for both residents and tourists.

Key Features:

Dune Bashing:

A thrilling highlight of the desert safari is dune bashing, an exhilarating off-road experience where skilled drivers navigate the sandy dunes in 4x4 vehicles, providing an adrenaline-pumping ride.

Camel Riding:

To capture the essence of traditional desert travel, camel riding is often included in the safari. Visitors can enjoy a leisurely camel ride and gain a unique perspective of the desert landscape.

Sunset Views:

The desert safari offers a spectacular opportunity to witness the breathtaking sunset over the dunes. The shifting hues of the sand and the golden glow of the setting sun create a mesmerizing panorama.

Cultural Activities:

Many desert safari experiences incorporate cultural activities, such as henna painting, traditional Arabic dress photography, and live performances of dance forms like belly dancing and Tanoura.

Desert Camp Experience:

The safari typically includes a visit to a desert camp where visitors can enjoy a buffet dinner featuring a variety of Arabic and international dishes.

The camp provides a comfortable setting for relaxation and stargazing.

Sandboarding:

Thrill-seekers can try sandboarding, gliding down the dunes on a board, offering an exciting way to interact with the sandy terrain.

Tourist Experience:

Cultural Immersion:

The Dubai Desert Safari offers a unique opportunity for cultural immersion, providing a glimpse into traditional Bedouin practices and the nomadic way of life.

Photography Opportunities:

The desert's stunning landscapes, the play of light during sunset, and the cultural activities at the camp create excellent photo opportunities.

Photography enthusiasts can capture the essence of the desert safari experience.

Travel Tips:

Wear Comfortable Clothing: Dress comfortably, considering the desert climate.

It's advisable to wear loose, breathable clothing and comfortable shoes suitable for sand activities.

Hydration: Carry sufficient water to stay hydrated, especially if visiting during the warmer months.

Sun Protection: Use sunscreen, sunglasses, and a hat to protect yourself from the sun.

The Dubai Desert Safari offers a dynamic blend of adventure, culture, and natural beauty, allowing tourists to escape the urban landscape and venture into the vast expanse of the Arabian Desert.

Whether seeking adrenaline-fueled dune bashing or a serene camel ride at sunset, the desert safari promises an unforgettable experience for those eager to explore the desert's mystique.

Dubai Aquarium & Underwater Zoo

History:

Dubai Aquarium & Underwater Zoo, situated within The Dubai Mall, opened its doors in 2008 as one of the largest suspended aquariums in the world.

With a vision to bring the wonders of the underwater world to the heart of the city, the aquarium has become a centerpiece attraction, captivating visitors with its immersive marine experiences.

Location:

The Dubai Aquarium & Underwater Zoo is strategically located within The Dubai Mall, one of the world's largest shopping and entertainment destinations. Its central location in downtown Dubai makes it easily accessible for tourists and residents alike.

Key Features:

Main Tank:

The centerpiece of the aquarium is the colossal Main Tank, which holds over 10 million liters of water. It is home to a diverse array of marine life, including sharks, rays, and a stunning variety of fish.

The acrylic viewing panel provides visitors with an up-close encounter with the marine inhabitants.

Underwater Tunnel:

The aquarium boasts a 48-meter-long walkthrough tunnel, offering a 270-degree view of the Main Tank. Visitors can stroll through the tunnel surrounded by marine life, creating a mesmerizing and immersive experience.

Underwater Zoo:

Adjacent to the aquarium is the Underwater Zoo, a fascinating space that showcases a wide range of species, including penguins, crocodiles, jellyfish, and more. The zoo introduces visitors to the unique ecosystems and behaviors of various aquatic creatures.

Interactive Experiences:

Dubai Aquarium & Underwater Zoo offers interactive experiences such as cage snorkeling, where visitors can safely dive into the main tank, and shark dives for those seeking a more adventurous encounter with marine life.

Educational Programs:

The aquarium is committed to education and conservation. It offers educational programs for schools and visitors, raising awareness about marine ecosystems and the importance of conservation efforts.

Tourist Experience:

Diverse Marine Life:

The Dubai Aquarium & Underwater Zoo showcases a stunning diversity of marine life, providing visitors with a comprehensive look into the wonders of the ocean.

Photography Opportunities:

The aquarium's design and lighting offer excellent photography opportunities. The vibrant colors of the coral reefs, the graceful movement of the rays, and the awe-inspiring presence of sharks make for captivating images.

Travel Tips:

Ticket Options: Consider purchasing tickets that include additional experiences, such as guided tours or special encounters with marine animals.

Visit Timing: Plan your visit during weekdays or non-peak hours to avoid large crowds.

Dubai Aquarium & Underwater Zoo is a testament to Dubai's commitment to providing world-class entertainment and educational experiences.

For tourists, it offers a captivating journey into the mysteries of the ocean, allowing them to explore the beauty and diversity of marine life without leaving the bustling city center.

Burj Al Arab

History:

Burj Al Arab, translated as the "Tower of the Arabs," stands as an iconic landmark in Dubai and a symbol of opulence and innovation. Officially opened in 1999, it was designed to represent the sail of a ship, reflecting Dubai's maritime heritage.

Developed by Jumeirah Group, Burj Al Arab has since become synonymous with luxury and is often recognized as one of the world's most luxurious hotels.

Location:

Burj Al Arab is situated on its own artificial island, connected to the mainland by a causeway. The strategic location off the shores of Jumeirah Beach enhances the hotel's exclusivity and offers panoramic views of the Arabian Gulf. Its proximity to other key attractions makes it a prominent feature of the Dubai skyline.

Key Features:

Distinctive Architecture:

The design of Burj Al Arab is a marvel, with its sail-shaped structure reaching a height of 321 meters (1,053 feet).

The use of reflective glass panels gives the building a mesmerizing appearance, especially during the day when it reflects the sunlight.

Sky-high Atrium:

The hotel boasts an impressive atrium that extends through the entire height of the building.

The atrium is adorned with vibrant colors and intricate patterns, creating a sense of grandeur upon entering the hotel.

Luxurious Accommodations:

Burj Al Arab offers exclusive and opulent suites, each spanning two floors and featuring panoramic views of the Arabian Gulf.

The hotel is renowned for its personalized service, including the provision of a private butler for each guest.

Culinary Excellence:

The hotel is home to some of the finest dining establishments in Dubai. Notable among them is the Al Mahara restaurant, known for its underwater aquarium setting and delectable seafood offerings.

The Skyview Bar:

Perched 200 meters above sea level, the Skyview Bar provides guests with stunning views of the cityscape.

It's a popular spot for enjoying afternoon tea or evening cocktails in a luxurious setting.

Helipad:

Burj Al Arab features a helipad that has been used for various high-profile events and stunts, adding to the hotel's allure and creating memorable moments.

Tourist Experience:

Afternoon Tea Experience:

For visitors not staying at the hotel, the Afternoon Tea experience at the Skyview Bar is a popular way to enjoy the ambiance and luxury of Burj Al Arab.

Reservations are essential for this iconic experience.

Photo Opportunities:

The exterior of Burj Al Arab, set against the backdrop of the Arabian Gulf, provides spectacular photo opportunities. Sunset and nighttime shots capture the building's illuminated beauty.

Travel Tips:

Reservations for Non-Guests: If you're not staying at the hotel but wish to experience its restaurants or bars, it's advisable to make reservations well in advance.

Dress Code: Burj Al Arab maintains a smart-casual dress code, so visitors should dress appropriately.

Burj Al Arab stands as a testament to Dubai's ambition and commitment to pushing the boundaries of luxury and architectural innovation.

Whether as a guest or a visitor, experiencing the grandeur of this iconic structure is an essential part of exploring the vibrant city of Dubai.

Dubai Frame

History:

The Dubai Frame, inaugurated in 2018, is a testament to the city's commitment to cutting-edge architecture and innovation.

Conceived by renowned architect Fernando Donis, the frame represents a symbolic bridge between Dubai's past and its vision for the future.

The structure's design reflects the aspirations of a city constantly evolving and pushing the boundaries of modernity.

Location:

Situated in Zabeel Park, the Dubai Frame commands a strategic location that provides panoramic views of both Old Dubai and the city's modern skyline. Its central position makes it easily accessible, becoming a must-visit destination for tourists seeking a unique perspective on Dubai's transformation.

Key Features:

Architectural Marvel:

The Dubai Frame is a colossal rectangular structure standing at 150 meters tall and 93 meters wide.

Its design is a blend of modern aesthetics and classical elements, featuring a sleek gold cladding on one side and a geometric pattern reminiscent of Arabian calligraphy on the other.

Sky Deck:

The Sky Deck, located at the top of the frame, offers breathtaking views of Dubai's contrasting landscapes.

Visitors can witness the historic neighborhoods of Deira and Umm Hurair on one side and the glittering skyscrapers of Sheikh Zayed Road on the other.

Glass-floored Skywalk:

One of the most thrilling features of the Dubai Frame is the glass-floored Skywalk, providing an exhilarating experience for those daring enough to walk on a transparent surface high above the ground.

It offers a unique perspective of the city below.

Exhibition Spaces:

The interior of the Dubai Frame houses immersive exhibition spaces that showcase the city's transformation from a small fishing village to a global metropolis.

Interactive displays and multimedia presentations provide a captivating journey through time.

Dubai Future Gallery:

A futuristic addition, the Dubai Future Gallery within the frame offers glimpses into the city's ambitious projects and innovations, providing visitors with insights into Dubai's vision for the future.

Tourist Experience:

360-Degree Views:

The Dubai Frame provides visitors with a 360-degree view of Dubai, offering a unique vantage point to appreciate the city's evolution and architectural diversity.

Photography Opportunities:

The frame's design and its strategic location make it an ideal spot for capturing stunning photographs. From day to night, the changing colors of the sky provide a dynamic backdrop for memorable shots.

Travel Tips:

Visit Timings: Consider visiting the Dubai Frame during sunset to experience the magical transition from daylight to the city's illuminated skyline.

Tickets and Queues: Purchase tickets in advance to avoid long queues, especially during peak hours.

The Dubai Frame stands as a living testament to Dubai's journey from its humble beginnings to its current status as a global city.

With its innovative design, panoramic views, and immersive exhibits, it offers tourists a captivating experience that bridges the rich history and the ambitious future of this dynamic metropolis.

Ain Dubai

History:

Ain Dubai, the world's largest observation wheel, officially opened on Bluewaters Island in October 2021.

 Its inception was part of Dubai's continuous effort to set new benchmarks in architectural innovation and provide residents and visitors with unique and awe-inspiring attractions.

Originally known as the Dubai Eye, Ain Dubai stands as an iconic addition to the city's skyline.

Location:

Ain Dubai is located on Bluewaters Island, a vibrant mixed-use development situated off the coast of Jumeirah Beach Residence (JBR). The island is easily accessible, with dedicated transport links connecting it to the mainland. This strategic location offers breathtaking views of the Arabian Gulf, the Dubai coastline, and the city's iconic landmarks.

Key Features:

Record-breaking Height:

Ain Dubai stands at an impressive height of 250 meters (820 feet), making it the tallest observation wheel in the world. Its colossal size ensures that passengers enjoy unparalleled views of Dubai's ever-evolving landscape.

State-of-the-Art Capsules:

The observation wheel features 48 spacious capsules, each capable of carrying up to 40 passengers. The capsules are equipped with climate control systems, ensuring a comfortable experience in Dubai's varying temperatures.

Spectacular Views:

Ain Dubai offers stunning panoramic views of the city's skyline, including landmarks such as the Burj Khalifa, Palm Jumeirah, and the Dubai Marina.

The unique location on Bluewaters Island provides a 360-degree view of the surrounding seascape.

Illumination and LED Displays:

As the sun sets, Ain Dubai transforms into a dazzling display of lights. The wheel is adorned with an intricate LED lighting system, creating mesmerizing patterns and colors that can be seen from miles away.

Entertainment and Dining Hub:

Bluewaters Island, where Ain Dubai is situated, has become a lively entertainment and dining destination.

Visitors can explore a variety of restaurants, shops, and entertainment options before or after experiencing Ain Dubai.

Tourist Experience:

Unforgettable Rides:

Riding Ain Dubai provides an unforgettable experience, offering a bird's-eye view of Dubai's landmarks and coastline. The slow rotation ensures ample time to capture photos and appreciate the scenery.

Bluewaters Island:

Beyond the observation wheel, Bluewaters Island offers a range of attractions, including retail outlets, upscale dining options, and pedestrian-friendly spaces. It's an ideal destination for a leisurely stroll or a day of exploration.

Travel Tips:

Book Tickets in Advance: Consider purchasing tickets online in advance to secure your preferred time slot and avoid waiting in line.

Visit During Sunset: Plan your visit during sunset to witness Dubai's skyline transition from day to night, creating a magical atmosphere.

Ain Dubai stands as a symbol of Dubai's commitment to pushing the boundaries of architectural and entertainment excellence.

As the latest addition to the city's skyline, it offers tourists an unparalleled experience, combining breathtaking views with the excitement of being atop the world's tallest observation wheel.

Dining and Culinary Experiences

Local Cuisine

Dubai's culinary landscape is a vibrant mosaic that mirrors the city's diverse cultural influences and cosmopolitan spirit.

From traditional Emirati dishes to international flavors, the local cuisine in Dubai is a gastronomic adventure that tantalizes taste buds and showcases the city's rich culinary heritage.

Traditional Emirati Delicacies:

Al Harees: A traditional dish prepared during special occasions, Al Harees is a slow-cooked blend of meat, wheat, and a pinch of salt. The slow-cooking process gives it a unique texture and flavor.

Machboos: Also known as Kabsa, Machboos is a fragrant rice dish infused with aromatic spices and typically featuring meat (often chicken, lamb, or fish). It's a staple in Emirati households.

Luqaimat: For those with a sweet tooth, Luqaimat are small, deep-fried dumplings drizzled with date syrup or honey. These bite-sized delights are popular during celebrations and festive seasons.

Street Food Extravaganza:

Shawarma: A ubiquitous street food, Shawarma consists of marinated meat (usually chicken or lamb) shaved off a rotating spit. It's often served in a flatbread with garlic sauce and pickles.

Falafel: Crispy on the outside and soft on the inside, Dubai's falafel is a popular vegetarian snack. Served in a pita or as part of a mezze platter, it's a flavorful option for those seeking a quick and tasty bite.

Global Fusion:

Dubai's cosmopolitan atmosphere has attracted people from around the world, resulting in a fusion of international flavors that cater to diverse palates.

Levantine Cuisine: With a significant Levantine community in Dubai, enjoy dishes like hummus, falafel, and shawarma that showcase the flavors of Lebanon, Syria, and Palestine.

South Asian Influence: Dubai's culinary scene is heavily influenced by South Asian flavors.

From biryanis and kebabs to flavorful curries, the city's Indian and Pakistani offerings are a treat for spice enthusiasts.

Seafood Extravaganza:

Given its coastal location, Dubai is a haven for seafood lovers. Fresh catches from the Arabian Gulf find their way to local markets and dining establishments.

Grilled Hammour: A local favorite, Hammour is a white fish often grilled and served with traditional Emirati spices. It embodies the essence of fresh seafood in Dubai.

Jumbo Prawns: Dubai's seafood markets offer an array of jumbo prawns prepared in various styles, from grilled to curry-based dishes.

Sweet Indulgences:

No culinary journey is complete without exploring the dessert options, and Dubai has a sweet tooth to satisfy.

Umm Ali: Often referred to as the "Arabian bread pudding," Umm Ali is a rich and comforting dessert made with layers of pastry, nuts, and sweetened milk.

Baklava: A sweet treat enjoyed across the Middle East, Baklava is made with layers of phyllo pastry, nuts, and honey or syrup, creating a delightful blend of textures and flavors.

Whether you're exploring the spice-scented markets, indulging in street food, or dining in upscale restaurants, Dubai's culinary scene promises a delightful and diverse experience.

From traditional Emirati dishes that reflect the city's heritage to global flavors that mirror its cosmopolitan nature, Dubai invites you to savor a feast for the senses.

Low-Budget Dining Restaurants in Dubai

Tips for Finding Low-Budget Dining in Dubai:

Explore Local Cafeterias: Look for local cafeterias and small eateries that are frequented by residents. These places often offer budget-friendly meals with an authentic taste of local cuisine.

Visit Food Courts in Malls: Dubai has numerous shopping malls with diverse food courts. Many of these food courts feature a variety of international and local food options at reasonable prices.

Try Street Food: Street food stalls and food trucks can be found in certain areas of Dubai. These vendors often offer affordable and tasty snacks. Areas like Al Muraqqabat and Al Karama are known for their street food scene.

Check for Daily Specials: Some restaurants offer daily specials or meal deals, which can be more budget-friendly than ordering à la carte. Keep an eye out for such promotions.

Look for Ethnic Cuisine: Explore neighborhoods with a high concentration of ethnic communities. You can often find small restaurants or eateries serving authentic and budget-friendly dishes.

Utilize Apps and Websites: Use restaurant discovery apps, travel forums, or review websites to find budget-friendly dining options in Dubai. Apps like Zomato, TripAdvisor, or Google Maps can provide user reviews and ratings.

Consider Buffet Options: Some restaurants in Dubai offer buffet-style dining, which can be cost-effective, especially if you have a hearty appetite. Look for buffets during lunch hours for potentially lower prices.

Remember that Dubai's dining scene is dynamic, and new establishments may open while others may close.

It's advisable to check recent reviews and local recommendations for the latest information on low-budget dining options in Dubai.

Nightlife and Entertainment

Dubai, often regarded as the "City of Gold," is equally renowned for its dazzling nightlife and entertainment scene.

From chic lounges with panoramic views to vibrant clubs pulsating with energy, Dubai offers a diverse spectrum of nocturnal experiences.

Luxurious Lounges and Rooftop Bars:

At.mosphere - Burj Khalifa: Located on the 122nd floor of the iconic Burj Khalifa, At.mosphere offers a luxurious and refined atmosphere. Guests can enjoy signature cocktails and gourmet cuisine while taking in breathtaking views of the city.

White Dubai: A fixture on the global nightlife scene, White Dubai is a high-energy nightclub known for its top-tier DJs, dynamic light shows, and a sprawling rooftop terrace.

Iris Dubai: Situated at the heart of the city, Iris offers a stylish setting with a terrace overlooking the skyline. It's a great spot for enjoying crafted cocktails and international beats.

Vibrant Nightclubs:

Cavalli Club: Nestled in the Fairmont Hotel, Cavalli Club is synonymous with glamour. The venue combines a restaurant, lounge, and club, offering an extravagant experience with its Swarovski crystal embellishments and cutting-edge music.

Base Dubai: Positioned in the Design District, Base Dubai is a massive open-air venue hosting international DJs and renowned artists. It's known for its immersive visual displays and electrifying music.

SoHo Garden: Located in Meydan, SoHo Garden is a trendy nightlife destination featuring a stylish outdoor space. The venue hosts various events, from live music to themed parties.

Cultural Experiences:

La Perle by Dragone: For a captivating evening, consider La Perle, a resident show at Al Habtoor City. Created by Franco Dragone, the performance combines acrobatics, aquatic feats, and cutting-edge technology.

Dubai Opera: Positioned in the heart of Downtown Dubai, Dubai Opera offers a sophisticated setting for live performances, including concerts, ballets, and theatrical productions.

Beach Clubs and Bars:

Zero Gravity: Perched by the beach, Zero Gravity is a lively beach club and bar that transforms into a vibrant party destination in the evening. It offers stunning views of the Dubai Marina skyline.

Barasti Beach: A popular beach bar located at Le Meridien Mina Seyahi Beach Resort, Barasti is known for its laid-back atmosphere, live music, and beachside setting.

Late-Night Dining:

Al Satwa Night Market: For a unique culinary experience, visit the Al Satwa Night Market. Open until late, it offers a range of international street food, reflecting Dubai's multicultural influences.

Eat & Drink Restaurant: Situated in the H Hotel, this restaurant stays open late and is known for its diverse menu, offering everything from Middle Eastern dishes to Asian fusion.

Events and Festivals:

Dubai Shopping Festival (DSF): If you're visiting in January, the Dubai Shopping Festival is not just about retail therapy; it includes concerts, entertainment shows, and fireworks.

Dubai International Film Festival (DIFF):
Film enthusiasts can attend DIFF, a prestigious event showcasing regional and international cinema.

Dubai's nightlife and entertainment scene cater to diverse tastes, offering a mix of glamour, cultural experiences, and laid-back beach vibes.

Whether you're dancing the night away in a chic club or enjoying a cultural performance, Dubai's after-dark offerings are as diverse as the city itself.

Keep in mind that Dubai has certain cultural norms, and it's essential to be aware of local regulations and respect the city's traditions while enjoying its vibrant nightlife.

Practical Tips and Safety

Safety Guidelines

Dubai, with its modern infrastructure and cosmopolitan atmosphere, is generally a safe destination for travelers. However, like any international city, it's essential to be mindful of local customs and adhere to safety guidelines to ensure a smooth and enjoyable visit.

The following are key safety tips for travelers exploring Dubai:

Respect Local Laws and Customs:

Modest Dress: While Dubai is modern and cosmopolitan, it's advisable to dress modestly in public areas, especially when visiting religious sites or local neighborhoods.

Public Behavior: Public displays of affection are frowned upon, and behaviors that may be acceptable in other cultures may not be appropriate in Dubai. It's essential to respect local customs and traditions.

Stay Hydrated and Sun-Protected:

Hot Climate: Dubai has a desert climate with extremely high temperatures, especially during the summer months. Stay hydrated by drinking plenty of water, wear sunscreen, and avoid prolonged exposure to the sun.

Appropriate Clothing: Choose lightweight, breathable clothing to stay comfortable in the heat. Protect yourself from the sun with sunglasses, a hat, and sunscreen.

Stay Informed About Local Guidelines:

COVID-19 Measures: Stay informed about any COVID-19-related guidelines and restrictions. Compliance with health and safety protocols, including mask-wearing and social distancing, is crucial.

Local Laws: Be aware of local laws and regulations, including traffic rules and alcohol consumption regulations. Dubai has strict laws, and ignorance is not typically accepted as an excuse.

Secure Your Belongings:

Pickpocketing: While Dubai is relatively safe, it's wise to keep an eye on your belongings in crowded areas and public transportation. Use anti-theft bags and wallets for added security.

Hotel Safes: Utilize hotel safes for valuable items, passports, and excess cash. Most hotels in Dubai offer secure storage facilities for guests.

Transportation Safety:

Seat Belts: Always wear seat belts when traveling by car. It's a legal requirement, and fines may be imposed for non-compliance.

Licensed Taxis: Use licensed taxis or reputable ride-sharing services. Avoid accepting rides from unmarked vehicles.

Emergency Numbers and Services:

Memorize Emergency Numbers: Familiarize yourself with emergency contact numbers in Dubai. The general emergency number is 999, and 998 is for police emergencies.

Healthcare Services: Dubai has a well-established healthcare system. Save the contact information for hospitals and clinics in case of emergencies.

Currency Exchange and Payment Security:

Authorized Exchanges: Use authorized currency exchange services to avoid scams. Most hotels and shopping malls have reputable exchange counters.

Credit Card Safety: Exercise caution when using credit cards. Use ATMs located in well-lit, secure areas, and keep your PIN confidential.

Cultural Sensitivity:

Photography Etiquette: Always seek permission before taking photographs, especially of individuals. Avoid taking pictures of sensitive areas like military installations and government buildings.

Friday Prayer: During Friday prayer (Jumu'ah), many businesses may temporarily close. Plan your activities accordingly.

Stay Informed About Local Developments:

Weather Alerts: Dubai occasionally experiences sandstorms and heavy rainfall. Stay informed about weather conditions and follow any advisories.

Local News: Stay updated on local news for any developments or events that may impact your travel plans.

By following these safety guidelines and exercising common sense, travelers can enjoy all that Dubai has to offer while ensuring a secure and memorable experience in the City of Gold.

Local Etiquette

Dubai is a city that seamlessly blends tradition with modernity, and respecting local etiquette is crucial for a positive and culturally enriching experience.

Embracing the following social norms will not only enhance your interactions with locals but also demonstrate your appreciation for Dubai's rich cultural heritage.

Dress Modestly:

Public Attire: While Dubai is diverse and cosmopolitan, it's respectful to dress modestly, especially in public spaces and religious sites. Women, in particular, should cover their shoulders and knees.

Beachwear: Save beachwear for the beach or pool areas. When away from these zones, wear more conservative clothing.

Greetings and Politeness:

Greetings: The traditional Arabic greeting is "As-salamu alaykum," meaning "Peace be upon you." Respond with "Wa alaykum as-salam."

Courtesy: Politeness is highly valued in Dubai. Address people with titles such as Mr., Mrs., or Dr., and always use "please" and "thank you."

Public Displays of Affection (PDA):

Avoid PDA: Public displays of affection, such as kissing and hugging, are generally frowned upon. Keep romantic gestures private.

Respect During Ramadan:

Fasting Hours: During the holy month of Ramadan, refrain from eating, drinking, or smoking in public places during fasting hours. Many restaurants and cafes will be closed during the day.

Modest Clothing: Dress conservatively during Ramadan out of respect for those observing religious practices.

Photography Etiquette:

Ask Permission: Always seek permission before taking photographs of individuals, especially locals. Avoid photographing government buildings and military installations.

Privacy: Respect people's privacy, and refrain from taking pictures of women without their consent.

Right Hand for Gestures:

Right-Handed Gestures: When offering or receiving something, always use your right hand. The left hand is traditionally considered less clean.

Shoes Off Indoors:

Homes and Mosques: It's customary to remove your shoes before entering someone's home or a mosque. Follow the lead of your host or the local customs.

Greetings During Friday Prayer:

Respect Friday Prayer: During the Friday prayer (Jumu'ah), many businesses may temporarily close. It's a significant religious observance, and visitors should be mindful of this when planning activities.

Haggling and Bargaining:

Souks and Markets: Bargaining is common in traditional markets (souks). However, maintain a respectful and friendly attitude during the process.

Alcohol Consumption:

Licensed Venues: Dubai has licensed venues where alcohol is served, but public intoxication is not tolerated. Consume alcohol responsibly and be aware of designated areas.

Tipping Etiquette:

Service Charges: Some restaurants and hotels include a service charge in the bill. If not, it's customary to leave a tip of around 10%.

Taxi Drivers: Tipping taxi drivers is not mandatory, but rounding up the fare is appreciated.

Public Behavior:

Public Spaces: Avoid loud or disruptive behavior in public spaces. Dubai is known for its cleanliness, and maintaining a calm and respectful demeanor contributes to this reputation.

Language:

English and Arabic: English is widely spoken, but learning a few basic Arabic phrases can be appreciated by locals.

By embracing local etiquette, you'll not only ensure a smooth and respectful interaction with Dubai's diverse population but also gain a deeper understanding and appreciation for the city's rich cultural tapestry. The warmth and hospitality of the people of Dubai will undoubtedly enhance your overall travel experience.

Health Precautions

Dubai, with its gleaming skyscrapers and vibrant lifestyle, is a city that welcomes millions of visitors each year. Ensuring your health and well-being during your stay is paramount.

Here are essential health precautions to consider while exploring the City of Gold:

Hydration and Sun Protection:

Extreme Temperatures: Dubai experiences high temperatures, especially during the summer months. Stay well-hydrated by drinking plenty of water throughout the day.

Sunscreen: Protect yourself from the intense sun with sunscreen, sunglasses, and a hat. Consider avoiding outdoor activities during the peak heat hours.

Safe Food and Water Practices:

Bottled Water: Stick to bottled or filtered water to avoid waterborne illnesses. Ensure that the bottle seal is intact before consuming.

Hygienic Food: Consume food from reputable establishments to minimize the risk of foodborne illnesses. Avoid street food if you have concerns about hygiene.

Health Insurance:

Comprehensive Coverage: Ensure that your travel insurance provides comprehensive health coverage, including medical emergencies and potential repatriation.

Pharmacies and Medical Facilities:

Licensed Pharmacies: Dubai has well-regulated pharmacies that offer a wide range of medications. Purchase medicines from licensed establishments.

Emergency Services: Familiarize yourself with the locations of hospitals and clinics, and save emergency contact numbers.

Dubai's healthcare system is of high quality, but it's essential to know where to seek assistance if needed.

Traveler's Diarrhea and Motion Sickness:

Preventative Measures: Consider carrying over-the-counter medications for traveler's diarrhea and motion sickness, especially if you plan to engage in desert safaris or other activities.

Fitness and Wellness:

Exercise Caution: If you have pre-existing health conditions, consult your healthcare provider before engaging in strenuous activities or extreme sports.

Wellness Facilities: Take advantage of the wellness and spa facilities in Dubai for relaxation and rejuvenation.

Safety During Desert Activities:

Guided Tours: If participating in desert safaris or other desert activities, choose reputable tour operators. Follow safety guidelines provided by guides.

Hydration: Carry sufficient water during desert excursions, and be mindful of the desert's challenging conditions.

Medication and Prescription Drugs:

Prescription Medications: If you are on prescription medications, ensure you have an adequate supply for the duration of your stay. Carry a copy of your prescription.

Customs Regulations: Familiarize yourself with Dubai's customs regulations for bringing medications into the country.

Fitness Centers and Outdoor Activities:

Fitness Hygiene: If using fitness centers, ensure that equipment is sanitized before use. Follow hygiene practices in communal areas.

Outdoor Safety: Engage in outdoor activities with appropriate safety gear and adhere to guidelines set by operators.

Mosquito Protection:

Mosquito Repellent: While cases of mosquito-borne diseases are rare, it's advisable to use mosquito repellent, especially during evenings and in outdoor areas.

Heat-Related Illnesses:

Recognize Symptoms: Be aware of the symptoms of heat-related illnesses, such as heat exhaustion and heatstroke. Seek shade and hydration if you experience any signs of distress.

Emergency Services:

Know Emergency Numbers: Memorize or save emergency numbers, including the general emergency number (999) and the contact information of your country's embassy or consulate.

By prioritizing your health and taking these precautions, you can enjoy your time in Dubai with confidence, knowing that you are well-prepared to handle any health-related situations that may arise.

Safe travels.

Conclusion

As we draw the final curtain on this Comprehensive Dubai Travel Guide, we reflect on the journey through a city that stands at the crossroads of tradition and innovation, where ancient sands meet towering skyscrapers, and where the spirit of hospitality resonates in every corner.

Dubai, a jewel in the heart of the Middle East, beckons travelers with its magnetic charm, promising an odyssey of cultural richness, modern extravagance, and unforgettable experiences.

This guide has sought to be your compass, navigating you through the labyrinth of Dubai's wonders, ensuring that every moment spent in this city of opulence is not merely a visit but an immersive voyage.

From the historical bastions of the Dubai Creek to the glittering heights of the Burj Khalifa, and from the timeless allure of traditional souks to the futuristic landscapes of Dubai Marina, we have unfolded the layers of a city that defies expectations at every turn.

Dubai, as portrayed in this guide, is not merely a destination; it's an amalgamation of dreams realized and ambitions met.

Whether you seek the thrill of desert adventures, the tranquility of wellness retreats, or the vibrant pulse of its nightlife, Dubai is a canvas painted with a myriad of possibilities.

As we conclude this guide, we encourage you to step into Dubai with open hearts and open minds. Embrace the local customs, savor the flavors of its diverse cuisine, and allow the city to weave its tales around you.

The journey may lead you to the iconic landmarks of Burj Al Arab and the Dubai Mall, or perhaps to the serene expanses of the Miracle Garden or the historical richness of Al Fahidi.

Wherever your path takes you, let Dubai be more than a destination—it's an experience etched into the fabric of your travel memories.

In this city of superlatives, where every ambition reaches for the sky, we hope this guide has equipped you with the knowledge to make the most of your time in Dubai.

From the practicalities of visas and transportation to the nuances of cultural etiquette, we've endeavored to provide a comprehensive resource that mirrors the dynamism and diversity that define Dubai.

May your journey through Dubai be a symphony of exploration, a tapestry woven with the threads of discovery, and a memory that lingers long after your footsteps have faded from its vibrant streets.

As you embark on your Dubai adventure, may every encounter, every sight, and every moment resonate with the essence of a city that continually reinvents itself while honoring its rich heritage.

Dubai awaits, not just as a destination, but as an immersive experience that transcends the ordinary. Let the spirit of adventure guide you, and may your Dubai sojourn be a chapter in the grand narrative of your travels, one that unfolds with wonder, enriches the soul, and leaves an indelible mark on your heart.

Safe travels, intrepid explorer, as you venture into the embrace of Dubai's enchantment.

May your journey be as extraordinary as the city itself, and may the memories you create here be nothing short of spectacular. Until we meet again, under the glistening skyline of Dubai, farewell and bon voyage!

Printed in the USA
CPSIA information can be obtained
at www.ICGtesting.com
LVHW090245030524
779236LV00016B/69